Apple Seed to Apple Orchard

How to Build Wealth Without Worry, Stop Hidden Leaks, and Live a Peaceful, Stress-Free Financial Life

Michael Kirkpatrick

Apple Seed to Apple Orchard
How to Build Wealth Without Worry,
Stop Hidden Leaks, and Live a Peaceful,
Stress-Free Financial Life

A Product of Michael Kirkpatrick's Library

1st Edition 2025

Paperback ISBN: 978-1-0699049-0-4
Imprint: Michael Kirkpatrick

Printed in Canada.

Contents

Chapter 1
The Orchard Mindset

If what you thought to be true about money turned out not to be true, when would you want to know about it?

Imagine you had an apple tree in your backyard. If you were hungry, would you take an axe and chop down the whole tree just to get one apple? Of course not. You would simply pluck an apple from the tree and allow the tree to keep producing fruit for you and your family long into the future. You would never chop down your apple tree, yet when it comes to money, many families and business owners do the equivalent of chopping down their financial tree. They pay cash for major purchases to avoid paying interest but in doing so they permanently give up all the interest their money could have earned over the next several decades. They also give up control of their capital. The real question is: how do you keep your tree alive and producing for a lifetime, without ever chopping it down?

Planting the Metaphor

Think about that image for a moment. The apple tree isn't just about today's hunger; it represents tomorrow's meals, next year's harvest, and fruit for your children and grandchildren. Yet in the financial world, many families do the equivalent of grabbing the axe. They liquidate their capital, chopping down their tree, to meet immediate needs or to "play it safe" by paying cash.

The problem is subtle. On the surface, paying cash feels smart: no monthly payments, no interest expense, no obligations. But beneath the surface, something far more costly happens. When you pay cash, you lose the ability for that capital to keep compounding. You not only give up the apple in hand; you give up every apple that tree would have produced in the decades ahead.

This is where the orchard mindset begins: wealth is not built by chopping down trees for short-term gains. Wealth is built by planting, preserving, and nurturing trees so they produce fruit for life.

How Families Chop Down Their Trees Without Realizing It

Consider a simple story.

A business owner, let's call him Mark, built up $200,000 in savings over years of hard work. When it came time to buy new equipment, he paid cash. It felt good in the moment: no loans, no outside financing, clean and simple.

But here's what really happened: that $200,000, which could have kept compounding year after year, was gone in an instant. His orchard lost a tree. The equipment served its purpose, but the capital and decades of future harvests were gone forever.

Now imagine the alternative. Mark preserves his tree. He places his money in a structure that allows access without interrupting growth. He borrows against it, buys the equipment, and still lets the tree keep producing fruit. Over time, he has both the equipment and the growing orchard.

That's the essence of the ***Orchard*** **Mindset.**

The Quiet Cost of Cash

Many families don't see the cost because it's invisible. No one sends you a statement saying, *"Here's the interest you could have earned but forfeited."* Yet that cost is real. Every time you chop down a tree, you give up not only today's fruit but the next 10, 20, or 30 years of harvest.

Ask yourself:

- What would your capital be worth if it could compound without interruption?
- How much opportunity is lost each time you deplete savings for a purchase?
- How would your future look if your orchard kept growing while you still had access to your money today?

The orchard mindset insists on asking these questions. Because once you see the hidden cost of chopping down your trees, you can't unsee it.

The Bucket with Holes Connection

At the same time, it's not just about keeping your tree alive. You also need to guard against leaks. Picture your financial life as a bucket. Water flows in from many sources: income, business profits, investment returns, dividends, rental income, and more. Families and business owners often ask, "What's the most efficient way to fill the bucket?" Yet at the same time, money is draining out unnecessarily and unknowingly through hidden holes.

- **Taxes:** the steady drip that pulls money out every year.
- **Negative returns:** market downturns that punch bigger holes in your bucket.
- **Wealth transfers:** money flowing out of your family's hands and out of your control, often permanently. These can be obvious like debt interest payments, unnecessary fees, or overspending, or subtle like the opportunity cost of letting cash sit idle.

Even when families pour more in, chasing higher returns, timing the market, or buying the next hot product, the leaks remain. The problem isn't the inflow. The problem is the outflow.

The orchard mindset recognizes both truths: preserve your trees and plug the holes. Do that, and your orchard flourishes. Your bucket fills. And peace of mind finally replaces financial stress.

A Better Way of Thinking About Wealth

Traditional advice tells us to maximize returns, pay cash whenever possible, pay down your mortgage as fast as possible, and defer taxes to a future date. But what happens if you end up staying in a high tax bracket or if tax rates rise? What happens when markets fall the very year you need ready access to cash? What happens when an opportunity comes knocking and your capital is gone because you chopped down the tree?

The orchard mindset rejects these short-term fixes.

Instead, it asks:

- How can I keep my tree producing year after year?
- How can I ensure my money compounds without interruption?
- How can I access what I need, when I need it, on my terms, without destroying my future harvest?

This way of thinking is not about products. It's not about the next "hot" investment. It's about stewardship. It means treating your capital as something to be cultivated, protected, and preserved.

An Invitation to Stewardship

Imagine standing in your orchard ten years from now. Instead of stumps, you see rows of strong trees, each one producing fruit season after season. Emergencies don't scare you, because you know you can borrow against the strength of your orchard without cutting it down. Opportunities excite you, because you have liquidity and control. And your children walk with you among the trees, knowing they'll inherit not just the harvest but the knowledge and system that keeps producing it.

That's the vision of the orchard mindset.

It is not a fantasy. It is a choice. A choice to stop chopping down trees, to stop draining buckets, and to begin preserving and nurturing the capital you've already worked so hard to earn.

Pause for a moment. Ask yourself:

- Where in your financial life have you been chopping down trees for a quick harvest?
- What would be different if your capital had been left to grow, uninterrupted, for the last ten years?
- How would your stress level change if you knew your orchard was always growing, no matter what markets or tax rules did?

Write down one instance, just one, where you chopped down your apple tree. Then imagine the orchard that could have grown if you had kept it alive.

This isn't an exercise in regret. It's an invitation to see clearly. Once you understand the real problem, the solution becomes obvious.

The orchard mindset is just the beginning. It reframes wealth from something you chase to something you cultivate. It teaches us not to chop down our apple tree for one apple, but to preserve the tree for a lifetime of harvest.

In the next chapter, *What We've Been Taught (and Why It's Failing Us)*, we'll look closely at the beliefs that led so many families to pick up the axe in the first place. You'll see how mainstream financial wisdom, often repeated without question, has been quietly undermining your orchard. And once you recognize these patterns, you'll be ready to embrace a better way.

Your orchard is already growing. Every dollar you earn, every bit of capital you preserve, is a seed. The question is whether you'll chop it down for a one-time benefit or let it grow into something lasting.

Once you choose the orchard mindset, everything changes. You stop asking, "What's the best investment product?" and start asking, "How do I keep my tree alive and producing for generations?"

And that is the first step to building wealth without worry, stopping hidden leaks, and living a peaceful, stress-free financial life.

Chapter 2
What We've Been Taught (and Why It's Failing Us)

The Comfortable Story We've All Heard

Picture this: A family, let's call them the Johnsons, sits across from a financial planner at their local office. They're diligent, responsible, and committed to "doing the right thing." They've worked hard, saved consistently, and followed the advice they were always told to trust.

The plan sounds familiar:

- Stay out of debt.
- Contribute as much as possible to registered accounts.
- Pay down debt aggressively to avoid interest.
- Invest in a portfolio of stocks and bonds.
- "Ride out" the market's ups and downs.
- Hope you retire in a lower tax bracket.
- Hope tax rates will be lower when you need to access your cash.

The Johnsons nod along. They've heard this before from their parents, from friends, from articles, and from financial entertainers on television. It feels safe, even virtuous. They leave the office believing they are set up for success.

And yet, despite doing all this, they still feel unsettled. They look at their statements, read about tax changes in the news, and wonder: If we're doing everything "right," why does it still feel so uncertain? Why are we still asking if there's a better way?

How Financial Wisdom Became Conventional

Much of what we've been taught about money sounds like common sense. It's been repeated so many times, it's easy to accept as truth:

- "Defer taxes whenever you can."
- "It's smart to pay cash, avoid interest at all costs."
- "You can't time the market, so just stay invested and ride it out."

These beliefs didn't appear overnight. They were passed down from earlier generations who lived through different economic realities. They were reinforced by governments promoting savings programs and institutions selling investment products. They were repeated by financial entertainers who make complex strategies sound simple.

Over time, these ideas hardened into rules. Rules that seemed safe to follow. For many, they became the financial equivalent of gravity: unquestionable, invisible, always there.

But here's the uncomfortable truth: many of these rules no longer serve us. In fact, some quietly work against us.

Why the Old Rules Fail

Let's take them one by one.

1. Deferring Taxes Is Always Smart

The logic sounds good: don't pay tax today, because your tax rate will be lower in the future.

But who controls future tax rates? Not you. Not me. Not your advisor. Tax policy is a moving target. And if rates rise, you could end up paying more than if you had settled the tax bill earlier.

Imagine sitting at a boardroom table. A contract is slid across to you. The terms look fine, except the price will only be revealed 20 or 30 years from now. Would you ever sign that deal? Of course not. Yet that's exactly what happens when families defer taxes without question, they hand over control and hope the future rules are kind.

Let's assume tax rates don't change. Is your dream really to work your whole life only to retire into a lower tax bracket? For some, that might be the plan, and that's perfectly fine. But for many, the real goal is the opposite: to retire with the same lifestyle, or an even better one. After all, who wakes up in the morning and says, *'You know what I want in retirement? Less income and fewer options.'*

2. Pay Cash to Avoid Interest

This one feels almost moral. Paying cash equals discipline. Debt equals danger.

But here's what no one tells you: when you pay cash, you don't avoid interest. You simply give up the interest your money could have earned if it had stayed compounding. You either pay interest to someone else, or you give up interest your own money could have earned.

Paying cash often means chopping down your apple tree for a one-time harvest, losing decades of future growth.

3. Ride Out the Market

This is the rallying cry of the investment world: "Stay the course."

But let's be honest. Riding out market swings is easy to say, but much harder to live through. Watching your wealth shrink in a downturn creates stress, uncertainty, and sometimes panic-driven decisions. And even if you hold steady, timing matters. Retiring during a market decline can permanently damage your long-term wealth, no matter how patient you are.

"Riding it out" doesn't guarantee peace of mind. For many, it guarantees stress.

Why Families Feel Stuck

Think about it:

- They defer taxes, only to face a bigger bill later.
- They pay cash, only to lose decades of compounding.
- They stay in the market, only to feel whiplashed by volatility.

No wonder so many families are asking: If I've followed all the rules, why doesn't it feel like I'm winning?

It's because these strategies address symptoms, not root causes. They ignore the real problems: taxes draining wealth, negative returns breaking compounding, and constant transfers of capital out of the family system.

The leaks remain. The bucket keeps draining. The orchard keeps being chopped down.

The Golf Club vs. The Swing

Here's a different way to see it.

Imagine a golfer frustrated with their game. Every season, they buy the latest club, a driver promising more distance, an iron designed for precision, a putter with better balance. They invest in equipment, hoping this time it will improve their game.

Sound familiar? That's how most people treat money. They search for the latest product, the next fund, the newest account, the hot "can't-miss" investment. They believe the club will fix their financial game.

But here's the truth: it's not the club. It's the swing. Your financial mindset, strategy, and discipline matter far more than the latest product. A great golfer with an old club can outperform a poor golfer with the newest technology. In the same way, a family with the right financial swing can outperform one chasing every new product.

The orchard mindset you saw in the last chapter is the swing. It's about protecting the tree, preserving compounding, and controlling the finance function in your life. The products: registered accounts, mutual funds, tax shelters, private equity, and crypto, are just clubs. Without the right swing, they won't save you.

The Emotional Cost of the Old Rules

This isn't just about math. It's about how it feels to live under the old rules.

Watching markets drop and wondering if your retirement plans are evaporating.

Reading about tax changes and realizing your carefully crafted plan no longer works.

Paying cash for a purchase, then facing an emergency with no liquidity. These aren't just financial inconveniences. They are stress-inducing, sleep-stealing realities. Families and business owners can feel out of control, vulnerable, and frustrated, despite doing everything they were told to do.

Peace of mind doesn't come from riding out storms. It comes from building a system where storms don't matter.

Take a moment. Write down the three biggest pieces of financial advice you've ever followed. Maybe it was "contribute to your registered account," "pay off your mortgage early," or "invest in stocks and bonds and ride out the ups and downs."

Now ask yourself:

- Did this advice give me more control or less?
- Did it provide peace of mind, or add more uncertainty?
- Did it build my orchard, or chop it down?

Then ask the central questions:

- If what you thought to be true about money, turned out not to be true, when would you want to know?

For most people, the answer is simple: ***right now.*** This exercise isn't about regret. It's about clarity. It's about recognizing where the old rules have quietly failed you so that you're open to a better way.

A Better Approach

We've now seen how conventional wisdom, the advice you've been taught to trust, can quietly undermine your financial future. It's not because you've done anything wrong. It's because the rules themselves are flawed.

In the next chapter, *From Return-Chasing to Control-Building*, we'll explore one of the most seductive but destructive habits in wealth building: chasing higher returns. You'll see how the red balloon of promised returns lures families off a financial cliff, and why the key to lasting wealth isn't chasing more, it's controlling what you already have.

The fact that you're reading this book means you're already questioning the old rules. You're already asking: *Is there a better way?* That willingness to challenge what you've been taught is the seed of transformation.

Once you see that the swing matters more than the club, that preserving your orchard matters more than chopping it down, you can never go back.

And that clarity, the courage to rethink your thinking, is what elevates families who are already doing well into true Wealth Creators.

Chapter 3

From Return-Chasing to Control-Building: Red Balloons, Cliffs, and the Math of Losses

The Temptation of the Red Balloon

Picture this: you're standing in an open field. Floating just ahead of you is a bright red balloon with '10% Return' written across it. It drifts upward, just out of reach. The promise is tempting; if you could just grab it, maybe you'd move even further ahead, stacking more on top of the success you already have.

So you start running. Eyes locked upward, you chase harder. The balloon rises higher, pulling your gaze further and further away from the ground beneath your feet. The faster you run, the less you notice the cliff edge approaching.

Then, suddenly, the ground disappears. You've run straight off a financial cliff and suffered a financial loss. That single step wipes out years of effort.

This is the return-chasing trap. Families and business owners spend years running after the balloon: the hot new stock, the latest fund, or the shiny alternative investment. The temptation is always the same: 'This one will finally fix it.' Yet what they don't see is that every chase risks a sudden fall, a negative return that interrupts compounding and knocks their portfolio off course.

The balloon is the promise of higher returns. The cliff is the reality of losses. The fall is the broken compounding that comes when wealth is exposed to risk.

Why Chasing Feels So Natural

Conventional wisdom has conditioned us to believe that the answer to financial stress is always "more." More growth, more return, etc. The media parades success stories of investors who "got in early" or "timed it right." Financial entertainers shout about which golf club, or investment product, is the one we're missing.

For many families, it feels responsible to chase higher returns. After all, isn't "more growth" supposed to be the goal? Yet hidden beneath this thinking is a dangerous assumption: that if we simply stack enough good years together, we'll come out ahead.

But wealth doesn't grow like that. The math of loss works differently. One bad year doesn't just cancel out one good year. It permanently disrupts compounding, like losing a tree in your orchard. One moment of damage erases decades of future harvests.

The Math of Losses

Let's start with a simple example. Imagine you have $100,000 invested. In the first year, your portfolio drops by 30%. You're down to $70,000.

What do you need the next year just to get back to even?

A 30% gain? No.

You need a 43% gain.

That's the math of recovery. Losses don't just take money, they take time. And time is the one resource you can never replace.

Steady vs. "Mostly Better"

Now, let's compare two different growth paths over ten years, both starting with $10,000:

- **Path A:** A steady 5% every single year.
- **Path B:** An 8% return every year, except for a= single year of –20% which occurs in year 1.

Here's how it plays out:

Year	Steady 5% Growth	8% Growth with One -20% Year
1	$10,500	$8,000
2	$11,025	$8,640
3	$11,576	$9,331
4	$12,155	$10,078
5	$12,763	$10,884
6	$13,401	$11,755

7	$14,071	$12,695
8	$14,775	$13,711
9	$15,513	$14,807
10	$16,289	$15,992

At the end of 10 years, the steady 5% leaves you with $16,289. The "mostly better" path with 8% most years but one bad year leaves you with less: $15,992.

The lesson? Even though nine out of ten years looked "better," the single year of loss erased the advantage.

By the way, it doesn't matter if the bad year comes early, late, or in the middle. The result is the same, and the damage is permanent.

The Sequence of Returns Trap

Losses become even more destructive when you need to withdraw money.

Imagine two retirees, each starting with $1,000,000 and withdrawing $40,000 every year. Both average the same 5% return over five years but one of them suffers negative returns early on.

Scenario A: Steady 5% Growth

Year	Return	End Balance
1	+5% → $1,050,000 – $40k	$1,010,000
2	+5% → $1,060,500 – $40k	$1,020,500
3	+5% → $1,071,525 – $40k	$1,031,525

4	+5% → $1,083,101 – $40k	$1,043,101
5	+5% → $1,095,256 – $40k	$1,055,256

Scenario B: Volatile 5% Average

Year	Return	End Balance
1	–10% → $900,000 – $40k	$860,000
2	–5% → $817,000 – $40k	$777,000
3	+10% → $854,700 – $40k	$814,700
4	+15% → $936,905 – $40k	$896,905
5	+15% → $1,031,441 – $40k	$991,441

Result after 5 years:

- Steady growth: $1,055,256.
- Volatile path: $991,441.

That's a $63,815 gap, even though the average return was the same.

Why? Because early losses broke compounding and withdrawals locked in the pain.

This is called sequence of returns risk. And it can devastate wealth at the very moment you need it most.

Timing Risk: Brother vs. Brother

Consider this example. Two brothers with the same portfolio fully invested in the S&P 500:

- One retired in 1980. Over the next ten years, the market averaged **17.43% annually**. Every $1 grew into $4.99.

- The other retired in 2000. Over the next ten years, the market averaged **–0.95% annually**. Every $1 shrank to $0.91.

Same portfolio. Same plan. The only difference was timing.

The first brother's orchard flourished. The second brother's orchard withered.

And here's the critical question: Can you control what the market will do in the year you need money? Of course not. And that lack of control combined with negative returns is a problem.

The Hidden Cost of Return-Chasing

Return-chasing isn't just destructive mathematically. It takes a toll emotionally and mentally.

- **Stress**: Constantly monitoring markets, second-guessing decisions, reacting to headlines.
- **Time cost**: Hours spent reading, researching, and worrying, with no guarantee of better results.
- **Opportunity cost**: Energy poured into speculation instead of strategy, family, or business.

For some, following markets feels like a hobby. For most, it becomes an exhausting distraction. And at the end of the day, chasing more rarely delivers more.

From Chasing to Control

Here's the breakthrough: **wealth isn't built by chasing returns. It's built by controlling the things you can control.**

You cannot control:

- The stock market.
- Tax rates ten years from now.
- Political or policy changes.
- When you might need ready access to cash for an emergency or opportunity

But you can control:

- Whether your capital continues compounding uninterrupted.
- Whether your system gives you liquidity, use, and control.
- Whether you rely on hope or strategy.

This is the pivot. Stop chasing balloons. Plug the leaks. Stop running toward cliffs. Cultivate your orchard.

The Control Question

Let's return to you for a moment.

Imagine you're preparing for the stage of life when you want more freedom, whether that's stepping back from your business, scaling down, or simply having options. You've worked hard to build wealth. You've saved, invested, and disciplined yourself.

But here's the question:

- Can you control what the market will do in the exact year you want to slow down?
- Can you control what tax rates will be when you retire or when you pass your wealth on to the next generation?

If the answer is no, then relying on return-chasing or a favorable tax policy is a gamble. And gambling is not a strategy.

Reframing the Path Forward

The truth is simple but powerful:

- One bad year erases many good ones.
- Sequence of returns risk can devastate a retirement plan.
- Timing is outside your control.

So the solution must be built on what you can control. That's the Wealth Creator's advantage: capital that compounds uninterrupted, stays accessible when you need it, and remains immune to market timing.

This chapter has been about proof: the math, the metaphors, and the wake-up call. The next step is about clarity, seeing how wealth is lost silently, not just through cliffs and balloons, but through leaks that drain your bucket year after year.

That's where we go next.

If you've ever felt the pull of that red balloon, the promise of "just one more hot investment," you're not alone. Every business owner and family has felt it. But now you know what's hiding beneath it: the cliff.

The good news? You don't need to chase. You don't need to gamble. You can shift from return-chasing to control-building. You can keep your orchard growing, your bucket filling, and your peace of mind intact.

Because the truth is this: the best investment isn't the one with the highest return. It's the one that pays the most when you need it most.

Chapter 4

Hidden Leaks: Taxes, Negative Returns, Capital Transfers

The Silent Drain on Wealth

Picture this: a business owner works long hours, the company is thriving, and accounts are growing. On paper, it looks like success. Income pours in year after year.

Yet even with growth, important questions linger:

- Is my money sitting in the right accounts?
- Is there something more I should be doing?
- What else can I do to protect and grow the wealth I've worked so hard for?
- Should I be spending more time managing and reviewing my investment accounts?

These aren't questions born of failure; they're questions born of stewardship. And often, the real issue isn't how much money is coming in, but how much is quietly leaking out through taxes, negative returns, and capital transfers.

These leaks are not dramatic explosions that capture headlines. They don't arrive with bells, whistles, or breaking news. They are subtle, persistent, and largely invisible until you pause to investigate. Like a dripping pipe behind the wall, they can cause enormous damage over time if ignored.

The leaks are:

1. Taxes.
2. Negative returns.
3. Capital transfers – money leaving your system permanently.

Let's examine each one closely.

Taxes – The Annual Drain and the Ticking Tax Time Bomb

Annual Tax: The Slow Leak

For those with taxable investment accounts, the leak is constant, though not always obvious. Each year, dividends, interest, and realized gains trigger tax slips.

But here's what's misleading: the portfolio statement doesn't show the tax. If your investments earn 10%, the report still shows 10%. Yet after the CRA takes its share, your net growth might be closer to 7%.

Why the disconnect? Because the tax isn't deducted from the account itself. You receive a T-slip, file your return, and pay the tax from your bank account.

This separation creates an illusion. Families don't link the tax payment to the portfolio that generated it.

They see the investment account "growing," while the true cost drains silently from another pocket.

Think of it this way: if your investment account actually subtracted the tax right on the statement, you'd see the bite instantly. Every season, a chunk of your orchard's fruit is gone before you could even taste it. Families wouldn't ignore that. They'd ask hard questions: *Why is this happening? Is there a smarter way? How do I stop losing so much fruit every year to tax?* The outrage would spark action, because once you see the leak, you can't unsee it.

But because the money to pay the tax bill comes from a different pocket, most never connect the dots. The orchard keeps producing, but fruit is carried off each year without fanfare.

This is the slow leak: not dramatic, but corrosive. Over decades, it quietly strips away enormous amounts of growth.

Walking to the back of the tax line

You or your business earns income. You step into the tax line, wait your turn, and pay your share. With what's left, your net income, you place money into a personal or corporate investment account.

But here's the catch: the moment you do, you've walked straight to the back of that same tax line. You'll queue up again, waiting to pay tax on every dollar of investment income those already-taxed dollars generate.

Each trip through the line takes more of your money, again and again. The absurd part? You've already paid tax once, but the system keeps sending you back for more. How many times will you keep lining up?

The Guest Who Always Shows Up

At every celebration of life, there's a chair reserved for a special guest. Not the grandchild carrying the family name forward. Not the friend sharing stories of laughter. The chair is reserved for a single, uninvited guest: the tax man.

He doesn't need an invitation. He waits until the end, and then he presents the largest invoice your family has ever seen. For many, that tax bill is shocking. After decades of saving and investing, much of what they worked for flows not to their loved ones or causes they care about, but to the tax man.

Deferred Tax: The Hidden Leak

Worse than the annual leak is the ticking tax time bomb.

In Canada, when someone passes away, the government assumes or "deems" that all their assets were sold that day. Every unrealized gain in a taxable account crystallizes. Every registered account, like an RRSP or RRIF, becomes fully taxable on the second death of a couple.

This is when the slow leak becomes a flood. Families who thought they had built an orchard to pass down watch as trees are cut down in one swoop.

Imagine tending trees for decades. You've watered them, pruned them, and guarded them from storms. At the very end, you expect your children to inherit a thriving orchard. Instead, the tax man arrives, taking not just apples, but entire trees. Growth that should have nourished future generations disappears.

Taxes are not just one leak. There are two:

- **Annual taxation**: the slow, steady drip that reduces growth each year.
- **Terminal taxation**: the sudden flood when the ticking tax time bomb explodes.

Both eat away at control, compounding, and ultimately peace of mind.

The Two Certainties

There are only two certainties in life: *death* and *taxes.* The question is: *what are you doing to plan for them?*

The reality is stark:

Canada's highest marginal tax rate exceeds 53%, meaning that for every additional dollar some families earn, more than half goes to the government.

The average Canadian family pays 45% of its income in taxes, a staggering increase from 33% in 1961.

Recent proposals to increase the capital gains inclusion rate show how quickly rules can change.

Wealth Creators don't leave their orchard exposed to such uncertainty. They build systems resilient to political and economic shifts.

Pause and ask yourself:

- Do I know how much tax my portfolio generates each year? Or am I fooled by statements that show growth while the real cost is paid elsewhere?
- Have I considered whether I should be paying tax on the seed or on the harvest?
- Do I understand how much tax liability is embedded in my accounts right now?
- Am I prepared for the terminal tax bill that arrives at death, often the single largest invoice of a family's life?

These questions may feel unsettling, but they open the door to clarity.

Shifting from Resignation to Control

Taxes are certain, but the size and timing of the bill don't have to be. Wealth Creators take a different path:

They minimize annual leaks by shifting money into tax-exempt environments.

They stop planting orchards in soil that guarantees a harvest-sharing agreement with the government.

They protect their trees from being chopped down at death, ensuring growth continues for future generations.

The goal isn't avoidance. It's stewardship, making sure the fruit of a lifetime's work nourishes your family, not just the tax system.

Another Leak in the Bucket

Even if you solved the tax problem, another silent leak remains: negative returns. One bad year can shatter compounding, erasing years of progress.

In the next chapter, *Negative Returns: Breaking the Compounding Chain*, we'll explore how market losses become another hole in the bucket, and why control, not return-chasing, is the only real answer.

You've planted seeds. You've built trees. You've nurtured an orchard. Don't let the tax man take the harvest, or the trees themselves.

By rethinking where your money grows, you can stop treating taxes as an unavoidable fate and start treating them as a challenge you can solve.

Plug the leak. Protect the orchard. And when the time comes to pass it on, let your legacy be measured not by what was lost to the tax man, but by what continues to grow for your family.

Chapter 5

Negative Returns: Breaking the Compounding Chain

The Gut Punch of Losses

Think back to the last time you opened a statement and saw your investments down 20%. Your heart sank. The questions came fast: *Should I sell? Should I wait? Will it come back?*

Losses don't just reduce numbers on a page. They create stress, uncertainty, and sleepless nights for families and business owners alike. And more importantly, they interrupt the most powerful force in wealth building: **compounding.**

This is the second great leak in the wealth bucket.

"Ride It Out" - The Conventional Teaching

For decades, the standard advice has been simple: markets go up and down, but over the long term they always recover. So just "ride it out."

The problem? That advice ignores how losses actually work. They don't simply balance out over time. A 20% loss isn't erased by a 20% gain. Losses interrupt the compounding. They take time away, and time is the one ingredient we can't replace.

And here's the bigger issue: you can't control *when* those losses will hit. They might arrive the year you want to retire, the year you need cash for a major purchase or to deal with an emergency or to act on an opportunity. Timing risk is beyond your control, yet conventional wisdom pretends it doesn't matter.

Losses Are Leaks, Not Inconveniences

In the last chapter, we looked at taxes as a slow and hidden leak. Negative returns are the second. And unlike taxes, which at least have some predictability, market losses strike suddenly and without warning.

In the math of losses section, we saw how damaging a single bad year can be. Remember the red balloon? Investors chase higher returns, eyes fixed upward, while ignoring the cliff in front of them. That cliff is a negative year, and when you fall, you don't just get bruised. You lose years of progress.

Let's recap the key lessons:

- **Loss recovery math**: A 30% loss requires a 43% gain just to break even. Losses hurt more than gains help.
- **Sequence of returns risk:** Two portfolios with the same average return ended up thousands apart when withdrawals started in a down year.

- **The one-bad-year test:** Nine years of strong returns couldn't offset one –20% year. The steady 5% path actually outperformed.
- **Brother vs. brother:** Same portfolio, different retirement years. One grew wealth fivefold, the other lost money. Timing, which is something you cannot control, made all the difference.

These weren't unlucky coincidences. They're the math of compounding. And they show why riding it out isn't a strategy. It's a gamble.

Proof Reframed as a Leak

Now, let's tie this back to the bucket with holes.

Income and savings pour into the top. Taxes are one leak. Negative returns are another. Even if you pour harder by earning more and saving more, the water drains out when losses hit.

And unlike taxes, which at least you can plan for, negative returns come like storms. You don't know when, you don't know how severe, and you don't know how long the recovery will take. All you know is that while the water drains, your compounding is interrupted.

This isn't about pessimism. It's about realism. Compounding is fragile. Once interrupted, it doesn't resume from where you left off; it starts again from a smaller base.

Reflection: What This Means for You

Consider these questions:

- Can you control when the next market downturn will happen?
- If it arrives the year you need money, how will that affect your plans?
- Do you know how many years it might take to recover from a single –20% year?
- Can you truly feel peace of mind if your financial future depends on timing you cannot control?
- These questions expose why negative returns are not just temporary setbacks. They are structural leaks that can derail even the best-laid plans.

Reframing Peace of Mind

Wealth Creators don't try to predict downturns. They don't chase balloons. They build systems that make volatility irrelevant.

Instead of worrying whether the market is up or down, they focus on control:

- Ensuring their money compounds without interruption.
- Having liquidity available no matter what the market does.

- Building structures that protect against losses rather than hoping to recover from them.

This shift is liberating. Suddenly, you're no longer glued to market news. You don't wake up anxious about headlines. Your orchard continues to grow, season after season, regardless of weather.

The Orchard Perspective

Negative returns are like a storm that strips fruit from your trees and can even damage the trees themselves. It doesn't just reduce this year's harvest; it weakens future seasons too. The orchard has lost time, and in some cases, lost trees.

Peace comes when you protect your orchard from storms. Not by trying to predict the weather, but by building resilience, so your trees keep growing and producing no matter what comes.

The Final Leak

So far, we've uncovered two of the three hidden leaks in building wealth:

Taxes: the slow and hidden drain.

Negative returns: the sudden storm that breaks compounding.

But there's a third leak. And for many families, it's the most devastating: capital transfers. Every time money leaves your system for a major capital purchase, you give up not only the money but also all the future growth it could have created.

In the next chapter, **Capital Transfers**: *Why Chopping Down the Tree Costs More Than You Think*, we'll see how giving up capital is like cutting down your apple tree for one big harvest. The tree is gone, and so is the future.

You've seen how powerful compounding can be. But you've also seen its weakness. Negative returns don't just sting, they shatter the chain. Years of growth vanish in an instant, and recovery always demands more than the loss ever took away.

You are not helpless. You don't have to gamble your future on timing the market. You can choose a system that protects compounding, that plugs the leak, and that lets your orchard grow regardless of the storms.

The peace of mind you seek isn't found in predicting returns. It's found in controlling the leaks.

Chapter 6

Capital Transfers: Why Chopping Down the Tree Costs More Than You Think

The Illusion of Paying Cash

Imagine this. A family buys a new car. They're proud because they paid cash. No payments. No lender. No interest.

That night at dinner, they celebrate: "We did it the smart way. We saved money by avoiding interest!"

But here's the quiet cost no one talks about: the moment they handed over that cash, they chopped down one of their apple trees.

Yes, they got the car. But they lost more than money. They lost control. They lost liquidity. They lost years of future harvests, interest and growth that tree could have produced for decades.

Whether they spent that cash on a car that depreciates or an investment that could fluctuate, the apple tree they cut down was their only asset guaranteed to keep compounding without interruption.

This is the third great leak in wealth-building: **capital transfers**.

What Feels Safe May Be Costly

For generations, families have been taught that paying cash is always the "smart" move. Parents and financial entertainers repeat it like gospel:

- "Avoid debt at all costs."
- "Paying interest is wasted money."
- "All debt is bad debt."

On the surface, it looks wise. It feels disciplined. It even feels like freedom. But in reality, it carries a hidden cost that most people never measure.

Here's the truth: we finance everything we buy.

- If we borrow, we pay interest to someone else.
- If we pay cash, we give up the interest our own money could have earned.

Either way, interest is paid. The only question is: *who keeps the harvest: you or someone else?*

The Orchard Lesson

Let's bring back the orchard.

Your capital is your apple tree. The apples are the interest it produces. Over time, one tree can become an orchard, a legacy that feeds your family for generations.

Now imagine chopping down that tree to buy a car, a piece of equipment, or a vacation home. Sure, you got what you wanted. But the tree is gone. And with it, every apple it would have produced for the rest of your life.

This is what happens every time families liquidate capital or pay cash for major purchases. They destroy not only today's money, but tomorrow's growth as well.

Wealth Creators refuse to chop down their trees. They let them keep growing and find ways to enjoy the apples while the tree remains alive.

The Illusion of Debt Freedom

Take another common story. A couple pays off their mortgage early. They feel triumphant because they no longer have mortgage payments.

But in the process, they drained their savings, leaving themselves with no liquidity. When an opportunity comes or an emergency strikes, they have to borrow again, often at worse terms than before.

Did they win? Or did they simply trade one kind of obligation for another?

Debt freedom sounds good, but true freedom comes from control. If you give up all your capital to eliminate payments, you've lost flexibility. You've chopped down the tree that could have funded both the payments and future opportunities.

The Golden Rule of Control

There's an old saying: "*Those who have the gold make the rules.*" In wealth-building, *those with liquidity and control dictate the terms of their future.*

Capital transfers rob you of that control, leaving you dependent on others for financing.

By contrast, protecting capital means you always have options. Emergencies don't derail you. Opportunities can be seized. Family legacies aren't compromised by the absence of liquidity.

Pause here and consider:

- Have you ever paid cash for a car, home renovation, or business equipment?
- Did you feel proud of avoiding interest, only to notice later that your savings account or investments felt emptier than you expected?
- Looking back, what future growth did you give up by chopping down that tree?

Write these down. These are the real costs of capital transfers.

Why This Leak Is the Most Dangerous

Of the three leaks, capital transfers are the most overlooked, and often the most damaging. Here's why:

1. **They feel like wins.** Paying cash gives an immediate sense of accomplishment. Families

rarely pause to calculate what they lost. No one mails them a statement showing how much interest that money could have earned over the next 20 years, or reminding them that by paying cash, they've permanently given it up.

2. **They interrupt growth.** Taxes nibble each year, negative returns strike occasionally, but chopping down trees destroys growth permanently.

3. **They erode liquidity.** Once the cash is gone, flexibility vanishes. Emergencies or opportunities force families back into external borrowing.

This leak feels safe, but it leaves families exposed and perpetually starting over.

Reframing the "Smart Move"

It's not that paying cash is bad. It's that it's incomplete.

Yes, you avoided paying interest to someone else. But you also gave up interest you could have earned. You surrendered control of your capital.

The real smart move is this: keep your tree growing. Borrow against it when needed. Let it keep producing fruit even while you enjoy the purchase.

This way, you have the car *and* the compounding. The expansion *and* the orchard. The lifestyle *and* the legacy.

From Discipline to Stewardship

Here's the critical identity shift:

- Consumers see paying cash as discipline.
- Wealth Creators see preserving capital as stewardship.

Discipline matters, but stewardship multiplies. Preserving the tree ensures the orchard survives and thrives, not just for today, but for generations.

Ask yourself:

- Which purchases in my life have chopped down trees?
- How would things look today if I had preserved that capital and let it keep compounding?
- What would change if, from this point forward, I refused to chop down any more trees?

These reflections mark the turning point from consumer to Wealth Creator.

We've now identified all three leaks:

1. **Taxes**: the slow drain and ticking time bomb.

2. **Negative returns**: the sudden break in the compounding chain.
3. **Capital transfers**: chopping down the tree itself.

Together, these leaks explain why so many families, despite their success, question whether their wealth is truly optimized. They're not failing; they're simply seeing signs of inefficiency that raise the question: "is there a better way?" The first step is seeing the problem clearly, because if we don't understand the problem, the solution won't do us any good.

The good news? Every leak can be plugged. And there is far more opportunity in avoiding losses than in chasing returns. Once the holes are sealed, the water you're already pouring in finally begins to fill the bucket naturally, steadily, and without extra effort.

In the next section, we'll explore the tool and the mindset shift that transforms these realizations into action. You'll see why chasing higher returns isn't the answer, and how plugging the leaks is the true path to wealth without worry.

You've worked too hard to keep chopping down trees.

Every dollar of capital you've built is a seed, a tree, an orchard waiting to grow. Don't destroy it for a short-term purchase. Preserve it. Let it compound. Use it wisely without losing it.

Wealth without worry isn't about deprivation. It's about preservation, keeping your orchard alive so it can feed you, your family, and generations to come.

The trees you protect today will be the legacy your children and grandchildren inherit tomorrow.

Chapter 7
What the Ideal Account Would Look Like

"There's Always a Catch"

If you've ever sat across from an accountant or financial advisor reviewing different types of accounts, you've probably heard some version of these conversations:

- "This account is tax-advantaged, but your money is locked away."
- "This one gives you access, but you'll pay tax every year."
- "This one grows quickly, but it's exposed to the markets."
- "This one is stable, but the returns are low."

Every option seems to come with a catch.

That's why so many families feel like they're settling, choosing the least-bad account instead of the best one.

But what if there *was* a perfect account? One that solved the real problems you face: taxes, negative returns, and capital transfers, while still giving you liquidity, use, and control of your money?

Before I tell you what that account is, I want you to imagine it for yourself.

Why Current Accounts Fail Us

Let's take a quick tour through the usual suspects.

Registered Accounts (like RRSPs or similar vehicles)

They offer a tax break today, but at a cost: you give up liquidity and control. Every withdrawal is fully taxable. And the whole strategy rests on one shaky assumption, that you'll be in a lower tax bracket in the future. But what if you're not? What if tax rates rise instead? Deferral can easily mean paying more, not less.

Taxable Accounts

You can access the money, but every year the taxman takes a bite. Dividends, interest, and capital gains all trigger tax slips that quietly reduce your real growth. And when you pass away, the embedded gains trigger the largest tax bill your family will ever face.

Holding Corporations

Many business owners use them, but here too investment income is taxed annually, and a silent tax liability grows year after year.

Traditional Savings or GICs

They are safe, but the growth is painfully low and often does not even keep up with inflation.

Market Investments

Potential for high returns, but no protection against volatility. One bad year can break decades of compounding.

Every one of these accounts forces a trade-off. Safe but stagnant. Liquid but taxable. High-growth but risky.

The result? Families feel like no matter where they put their money, they're losing ground somewhere.

Imagine a Perfect Account

Now, let's do something different. Instead of asking what accounts exist, let's imagine what the *ideal* account would look like.

If you could design the perfect place to store wealth for yourself, your family, and your business, what would it need to do?

Take a moment. Picture it in your mind.

Would it:

- Be tax-exempt?
- Grow every single day, and never move backward?
- Stay liquid so you could access capital whenever you needed it?
- Continue compounding even if you borrowed against it?
- Offer stability and peace of mind through every stage of life?

- Have a long, proven history of reliability?

That's the thought exercise we're about to walk through.

Step 1 – It Must Be Tax-Exempt

If taxes are the first leak, then the perfect account must solve it.

Ask yourself: why would you put money into a place where the government takes a slice every year, charges you again whenever you access it, and reserves the right to take the largest piece when you pass away?

An ideal account would allow your money to grow free from annual taxation. No slips. No hidden liabilities building in the background. No ticking tax time bomb waiting for your heirs.

Every dollar of growth would belong to you and your family.

Step 2 – It Must Be Safe from Negative Returns

If negative returns are the second leak, then safety is non-negotiable.

The perfect account would not gamble your future on markets. It would rise every day, come rain or shine. No volatility. No sequence of returns risk. No "retirement gamble" of wondering what the markets will be doing the year you need your money.

Even if the world economy wobbles, this account would remain steady.

Step 3 – It Must Stay Liquid

If capital transfers are the third leak, then the account must remain liquid.

Liquidity means you can access your capital anytime for emergencies, opportunities, or major purchases, without penalty. No handcuffs, no penalties. No forced waiting. No giving up control.

Imagine how different you would feel knowing that no matter what happens, you can always reach your money quickly and without hassle.

Step 4 – It Must Compound Uninterrupted

This is the key most accounts miss.

With traditional savings or investments, the moment you withdraw money, the compounding stops. But the perfect account would keep compounding even while you accessed funds.

Imagine borrowing against your account to buy a piece of equipment, a car, or an investment while your original capital keeps growing as if you never touched it.

That's uninterrupted compounding. It's like enjoying the apples while your tree keeps growing, season after season.

Step 5 – It Must Be Proven and Stable

Finally, the ideal account must have a long, tested history.

It's not enough to be new, flashy, or theoretical. Families want something they can trust, something that has delivered through wars, recessions, pandemics, and political changes.

The ideal account isn't experimental. It's timeless.

Pause here. Ask yourself:

- Which of these features matter most to me?
- If I could have an account that was tax-exempt, safe, liquid, compounding uninterrupted, and proven, how would that change the way I feel about my financial future?
- How would it change the way I teach my children about money?

Write your thoughts. This is where the vision of becoming a Wealth Creator begins to take root.

The Frustrated Business Owner

Consider John, a fictional business owner.

For years, John poured money into registered accounts. He liked the tax deduction, but every time he thought about using the money, he realized it would trigger taxes and penalties. He felt trapped.

So he shifted. He built up his personal investment account and his holding corporation's portfolio. At least there, the money was accessible. But every year, he wrote massive cheques to the CRA. It felt like running on a treadmill, with plenty of effort and no real progress.

To stay liquid, he also kept a pile of cash sitting in the bank. It was safe, but stagnant, earning next to nothing while inflation and taxes quietly eroded its value.

John was doing what everyone told him to do. But he always felt like he was playing defense, never offense.

Now imagine telling John: "What if there was an account that gave you tax-free growth, daily increases, full liquidity, uninterrupted compounding, and a 150-year track record of safety?"

How would that change John's life?

That's the power of imagining the ideal account.

Planting the Seed of Curiosity

At this point, you may be wondering: Does such an account really exist? Or is this just financial fantasy?

That's a good question, and exactly the one you should be asking.

Because once you see the features clearly, including tax exempt, safe, liquid, compounding, and proven, you will realize that anything less feels incomplete.

You wouldn't buy a house with no roof. You wouldn't plant an orchard without water. Why would you store your life's work in an account that can't protect it fully?

Up until now, we've focused on problems and mindset. You've seen the three leaks draining wealth. You've made the shift from chasing returns to building control. And now, you've imagined what the perfect solution would look like.

In the next chapter, *Introducing the Private Family Reserve*, we'll reveal the only tool that checks every box on this list. You'll discover why it's been hiding in plain sight, why so few families know how to use it, and how it becomes the cornerstone of the Wealth Creator's system.

Every great transformation begins with imagination.

Before an orchard grows, someone has to picture it. Before a family legacy takes shape, someone has to dream it.

You've now imagined the perfect account, one that protects, grows, and multiplies your wealth without leaks.

The next step is simple: discover it, name it, and make it your own.

Because when you find it, you'll no longer wonder where to put your money. You'll know you've found the safest, smartest, most powerful financial home for your wealth.

Chapter 8

Revealing the Tool: Introducing the Private Family Reserve

The Account You Imagined Is Real

In the last chapter, you pictured the perfect account. Tax-exempt. Growing every day. Accessible when you need it. Compounding uninterrupted, even while you borrow against it. Proven through time.

Here's the revelation: that account exists. It isn't theory, or a thought experiment, or financial fantasy. It is a carefully designed Participating Whole Life Insurance policy, structured not as an expense, but as a system. A system we call your **Private Family Reserve**.

This isn't the insurance product most people picture when they hear "whole life." In fact, most of what you've heard about insurance is incomplete at best and misleading at worst. This is not about death benefit alone. It's about creating a living, breathing account where your family's capital can grow without leaks.

Why the Reveal Matters

Let's pause and connect the dots.

You've seen the three leaks in your bucket:

- *Taxes:* the slow drain and the ticking tax time bomb.
- *Negative returns*: the storm that breaks compounding.
- *Capital transfers*: the self-inflicted wound of chopping down trees.

You've also imagined the features of the perfect account: tax-exempt growth, guaranteed increases, liquidity, uninterrupted compounding, and proven stability.

Now we bridge imagination and reality. The carefully designed Participating Whole Life Insurance policy is the only financial tool that solves all three leaks at once. It's not "just insurance." It's a structure for building and preserving wealth with control.

From Product to System

The first mental reframe is simple but critical: insurance by itself is just a product. A premium for a death benefit. A line item on a balance sheet.

But in the right hands, with the right mindset, the product becomes a system. A carefully designed Participating Whole Life Insurance policy isn't about what you buy. It's about how you use it. It provides a foundation that gives your family liquidity, access, and control of capital at every stage of life.

Premiums aren't just costs. They are deposits, dollars stored in a tax-exempt account.

Cash value isn't locked away. It is accessible, liquid, and can be borrowed against on your terms.

Growth isn't tied to markets. It's guaranteed, steady, and uninterrupted.

The death benefit isn't only for heirs. This tool gives you peace of mind today, supports your family with living benefits along the way, and ultimately transfers capital tax-free across generations, along with the knowledge of how to keep the orchard growing.

This is why we call it a Private Family Reserve. It functions like a family's own bank. Money flows in, compounds without interruption, remains available for use, and passes down across generations with unmatched efficiency.

Features That Solve the Leaks

Let's match the features directly to the problems.

Tax-Exempt Growth

The cash value inside a Participating Whole Life policy grows free from annual taxation. No T-slips. No cheques written from your bank account. No harvest taken each year. The orchard keeps its fruit, season after season.

Guaranteed, Uninterrupted Growth

Unlike market-based accounts, the value of a policy never moves backward. It goes up every single day.

Losses don't interrupt compounding. There is no "sequence of returns" risk. Your orchard grows steadily, storm or no storm.

Liquidity and Control

Policy loans allow you to access your cash value without withdrawing it. That means the cash values keep compounding even while you borrow against them. You can borrow to make a purchase, seize an opportunity, or weather an emergency, all without chopping down the tree. This is the *AND Asset*: You can add money to your policy *and* use it elsewhere at the same time.

Legacy Built In

The death benefit ensures a tax-free transfer to the next generation. Not just money, but the wealth creator mindset. The orchard doesn't end with you. It continues to grow for your children and grandchildren.

Compare the Options

Ask yourself:

- Does my registered account give me liquidity, or does it lock my money away?
- Does my taxable account show me the real cost of taxes, or does it hide them in a separate bill?
- Do my market-based accounts guarantee daily growth, or do they rise and fall beyond my control?

- When I need capital, do I chop down trees, or do I borrow against them while they keep growing?
- And when I pass away, does my RSP or taxable account hand my family a tax-free lump sum, or does it hand them a tax bill?
- When you compare, the differences are stark. Traditional accounts are designed with leaks. The Private Family Reserve is designed to plug them.

The Orchard Perspective

Think of your capital as apple trees. With most accounts, storms knock apples off, harvests are taxed away, or trees are chopped down entirely.

A carefully designed Participating Whole Life Insurance policy changes the soil your orchard grows in. The orchard is protected:

No storms break compounding.

No harvest is quietly taken.

No trees are chopped at death.

And even when you need capital, the orchard keeps growing while you use it.

This is not about chasing higher returns. It's about protecting your apple trees so they keep producing season after season.

Why You Haven't Heard This Before

If this tool is so powerful, why isn't everyone doing it?

There are several reasons:

- Financial entertainers emphasize rate of return, ignoring the leaks that matter more.
- Most advisors are trained to sell products, not systems. They push the next "club" instead of teaching the swing.

Misunderstandings about insurance run deep. People assume it's about death benefit only, or that it's too expensive. They've never been shown how a properly designed policy functions as a family's own bank.

The truth has always been hiding in plain sight. For over 100 years, Participating Whole Life Insurance policies have quietly delivered tax-exempt growth, uninterrupted compounding, and multigenerational transfers. What's been missing is the mindset: it hasn't been framed as the wealth-creation system it truly is.

From Discovery to Action

Now that you've seen the reveal, the next step is learning how to step into the role of Wealth Creator yourself. It's one thing to understand the tool. It's another to design and implement it for your family.

That's what the next section of the book is about. In *Becoming a Wealth Creator: The 7-Step Transformation*, you'll see exactly how to move from knowledge to action, a process anyone can follow, step by step, to reclaim control of the banking function in their lives.

You've spent years pouring water into a leaky bucket. You've endured taxes, losses, and capital transfers, often without realizing how much they were costing you. You've imagined a better account, and now you know it exists.

A carefully designed Participating Whole Life Insurance policy is the tool. The Wealth Creator mindset is the lifestyle, the foundation for your orchard, ensuring your trees continue growing, your fruit stays in the family, and your legacy endures.

This is the moment of clarity: you don't have to keep playing the old game. The account you imagined is real. The leaks can be plugged. The orchard can flourish.

Now, it's time to step into the transformation.

Chapter 9

Becoming a Wealth Creator: The 7-Step Transformation

Transformation Happens in Steps

Transformation is never a single leap. It happens step by step.

By now, you've seen the three most vexing problems that quietly erode wealth: taxes, negative returns, and capital transfers. You've seen why conventional accounts don't solve them, and you've discovered that there *is* a tool that can address these issues: a carefully designed Participating Whole Life Insurance policy, your Private Family Reserve.

But knowing is not the same as becoming. Knowledge alone does not plug the leaks or grow the orchard. What matters is transformation, the shift from consumer to Wealth Creator. And transformation follows a path.

This chapter gives you that path: seven steps that anyone can take to reclaim control of the banking function in their life, stop unnecessary losses, and grow wealth with peace of mind and legacy.

From Awareness to Action

Most families never move beyond awareness. They sense something's off, that their bucket isn't filling despite income or that their orchard isn't expanding despite effort, but they don't know what to do differently.

The purpose of this chapter is to replace that uncertainty with clarity. These seven steps are practical, proven, and repeatable. They don't depend on luck, timing, or speculation. They depend on mindset, process, and design.

Step 1: Education – Rethink Your Thinking

Every transformation begins with awareness, but Wealth Creators go further: they actively rethink their thinking.

This is why Nelson Nash, founder of the Infinite Banking Concept, always said: "If you don't understand the problem, the solution won't do you any good." Education means reading, listening, reflecting, and rethinking your assumptions. It means reading Nelson Nash's book *Becoming Your Own Banker*, studying our articles and videos, and engaging with mentors who understand the Private Family Reserve system. It means questioning long-held beliefs like:

- "Deferring tax is always good."
- "Markets always come back."
- "Pay cash to avoid interest."

The first step is humbling. It means admitting that what you've been taught might not be the whole truth. But once you see differently, you can't unsee.

Reflection Question: What financial "truth" have you accepted without question that might not actually serve you?

Step 2: Identify the Problems – Name the Leaks

Once your perspective shifts, the leaks become visible. You can't fix what you can't see.

- **Taxes** quietly drain wealth every year and explode at death.
- **Negative returns** break compounding, making timing a gamble.
- **Capital transfers** remove dollars from your system permanently, erasing future growth.

These are the three holes at the bottom of the bucket. Identifying them is liberating because it reveals the real enemy. It's not your effort. It's not your income. It's not your discipline. The problem is the leaks.

Reflection Question: Which of these leaks do you feel most in your own finances today?

Step 3: Update Your Net Worth & Tax Projections

Wealth Creators don't plan in the dark. They measure.

This step is about clarity. Updating your net worth shows exactly what you own, what you owe, and how money is flowing. Running tax projections reveals how much liability is embedded in your accounts and what your future tax bill could look like.

For many, this step is eye-opening. It's the first time they've seen their financial picture laid out clearly, not in product statements, but in a true balance sheet. And often, it reveals hidden risks: large deferred taxes, concentrated exposures, or capital potentially being eroded unnecessarily.

It's like walking into your orchard with a map. You can see which trees are healthy, which are vulnerable, and where weeds are choking growth.

Reflection Question: If you projected your taxes and wealth 20 years from now, would you be surprised by what you'd find?

Step 4: IFR Decision – Increase, Flatten, or Reduce Tax

One of the most powerful decisions Wealth Creators make is intentional tax planning.

There are three paths:

- **Increase**, your current and future tax liability.

- **Flatten**, your current and future tax liability.
- **Reduce**, your current and future tax liability through strategy and structure.

Most families don't realize they even have this choice. They assume the government dictates their tax outcome. But Wealth Creators understand they can design their orchard to manage tax exposure intentionally instead of reactively.

This decision alone can mean hundreds of thousands, sometimes millions, preserved for family legacy instead of lost to the tax man.

Reflection Question: Do you want your current & future tax liability to increase, flatten, or reduce?

Step 5: Introduce the Tool – The Private Family Reserve

At this stage, the tool itself comes into play.
A carefully designed Participating Whole Life Insurance policy is where capital is stored, tax-exempt, liquid, compounding daily, and transferable across generations.

This is not a product purchase. It's the soil for your orchard. It solves for the three leaks:

- **Taxes** → Growth is exempt from annual taxation.

- **Negative returns** → Value never moves backward.
- **Capital transfers** → Liquidity through policy loans allows use of money without chopping down trees.

By this point in the journey, the reader understands why this tool matters: it is the only structure that aligns with the Orchard Mindset and plugs every hole in the bucket.

Reflection Question: How would it feel to know your money is growing every day, tax-exempt, and available on your terms?

Step 6: Funding Strategy – Reallocate, Don't Add Burden

Wealth Creators don't see policy funding as an added expense. They see it as a choice to redirect dollars they already control. Every year, money is already flowing into registered accounts, taxable accounts, vacation savings, education funds, emergency reserves, renovations, business reinvestments, or cash purchases. The difference is where you direct it.

Will those dollars keep compounding for you, or will they leak away through taxes, volatility, and transfers?

Funding isn't about finding new money. It's about deliberately channeling the same dollars into the Private Family Reserve, where each one does two jobs at once: compounding tax-exempt inside the policy, while remaining accessible for business, purchases, or emergencies through policy loans.

Reflection Question: If your dollars could do two jobs instead of one, how much faster would your orchard grow?

Step 7: Design & Implement – Build Your Orchard

Finally, design and implementation. This is where the Private Family Reserve is tailored to your life.

- How much capital should flow into it annually?
- How should policies be structured for maximum liquidity and long-term growth?
- How can policies be layered across spouses, children, or corporations to build a multi-generational orchard?

Design is where vision meets reality. Implementation is planting seeds. It's where Wealth Creators stop talking about orchards and start cultivating them.

From here, the journey continues for life. Policies grow. Orchards expand. Families inherit not only money, but a system, a way of thinking about wealth that endures.

Reflection Question: What would it mean to know your orchard is growing steadily, compounding every day, ready to support both your lifetime and your legacy?

From Foundation to Maximization

With these seven steps, the transformation is complete. You are no longer a consumer of products, hoping the newest golf club will improve your game. You are a Wealth Creator, focused on your swing, stewarding an orchard, plugging leaks, and building a system that delivers clarity, control, and peace of mind.

But this is just the beginning. Once the foundation is in place, the Private Family Reserve can be maximized. Policy loans. Cascading life insurance. Rethinking mortgages. These strategies expand the orchard, pro tect it, and multiply its fruit.

That's where we go next, beginning with the *AND Asset*, showing how one dollar can do two jobs at once.

Recall that *"Transformation doesn't happen by accident. It happens step by step:"*

1. **Educate.**
2. **Identify.**
3. **Measure.**
4. **Decide.**
5. **Introduce.**
6. **Fund.**
7. **Design.**

Each step builds on the last, turning awareness into clarity, and clarity into action.

Wealth Creators don't wait for perfect conditions. They start. They plant. They cultivate. And they pass on orchards that outlive them.

Your orchard is waiting. The leaks can be plugged. The system is proven. The path is clear.

The only question is: are you ready to take your first step?

Chapter 10
The AND Asset: Dual Use of Every Dollar

Breaking the Either/Or Trap

Most people think about money in terms of trade-offs. *If I put it here, I can't put it there. If I save, I can't invest. If I pay down debt, I can't build wealth.* It's an either/or game, and the rules feel limiting.

But what if those rules weren't fixed? What if the very dollars you put to work in your Private Family Reserve could also be the same dollars you use to invest in real estate, expand your business, or seize opportunities? What if money could live in two places at once, compounding safely while financing your goals?

That is the AND Asset. And for Wealth Creators, this realization changes everything.

The Either/Or Mindset

Think about the financial crossroads families face every day:

- Should I invest in the market or keep cash on hand for emergencies?

- Should I buy equipment for my business or put money into savings?
- Should I pay off my mortgage early or fund my retirement plan?

Traditional advice says you must choose. Every decision feels like a sacrifice. Put money here, and it's gone from there. Grow the orchard, and you can't enjoy the fruit. Enjoy the fruit, and you risk chopping down the tree.

This either/or thinking creates stress and hesitation. Many families sit on the sidelines, paralyzed by the fear of making the "wrong" move. Others throw their money into whichever choice feels urgent, only to regret what they gave up.

The AND Asset frees you from this trap.

The Breakthrough: Money That Multiplies Its Use

With your Private Family Reserve in place, something powerful happens. Every dollar you contribute grows tax free inside your policy, compounding day after day, year after year. That alone is valuable. But here is the breakthrough: you do not have to lock that capital away. You can also access it through a policy loan without interrupting its growth.

In practice, this means *every dollar can*:

- Grow inside the policy (earning uninterrupted compounding).
- Be deployed outside the policy (to fund investments, opportunities, or purchases).
- One dollar. Two uses. Not an OR decision, but an AND strategy.

This is what makes the AND Asset so transformational. It reframes every financial choice. Instead of asking, *Should I do this or that?* you start asking, *How can I do both?*

The Business Owner's Expansion

Imagine a business owner named Daniel. He has $200,000 of retained earnings sitting in his corporation. If he invests it directly, he faces annual taxes on the gains. If he keeps it as cash, inflation erodes its value. And if he uses it to buy new equipment, the capital is gone, his orchard tree chopped down to get a single harvest.

Instead, Daniel funds his Private Family Reserve. His $200,000 now compounds tax-free inside the policy. A year later, he decides to expand his business with new equipment. Instead of draining the policy, he takes a policy loan. The $200,000 continues to grow inside the policy as if untouched. At the same time, the borrowed funds finance the equipment.

Daniel didn't face an OR decision. He didn't have to choose between growth and expansion. He did both. That's the AND Asset in action.

Why This Works

At first, it sounds almost too good to be true, until you understand the mechanics. Policy loans are secured by the cash value inside your Private Family Reserve. The insurance company lends you its money, using your policy as collateral, while your cash values continue to grow uninterrupted.

The result is convexity in action: your downside is limited (your capital is safe and compounding), while your upside is open (you can seize opportunities, invest, or cover emergencies). Instead of weakening your position, using your Private Family Reserve strengthens it.

The orchard stays alive. The apples keep coming. And you gain the flexibility to use today's fruit without sacrificing tomorrow's harvest.

The Mindset Shift

The AND Asset is more than a tool. It's a mindset. It trains you to think in terms of expansion, not sacrifice.

Instead of:

- *Should I save or invest?* → **You save and invest.**
- *Should I build wealth or finance my business?* → **You build wealth and finance your business.**
- *Should I preserve capital or take advantage of opportunities?* → **You preserve capital and take advantage of opportunities.**

This is why families who embrace the AND Asset often describe it as a sense of freedom. They no longer feel trapped by tradeoffs. Their decisions are no longer weighed down by scarcity. They operate from abundance, knowing their orchard keeps growing even as they enjoy the fruit.

Real-World Applications

The AND Asset shows up in countless ways:

Business owners can fund policies with retained earnings, then borrow against them to expand operations, buy equipment, or cover payroll during slow seasons.

Families can contribute to their Private Family Reserve, then use policy loans to fund a child's education or help with a down payment on a home, without interrupting long-term growth.

Investors can borrow against their policies to buy real estate, while their policy capital continues to compound untouched.

Each example reframes the question. It's no longer "Do I do this or that?" It becomes "How can I structure this so I can do both?"

Pause here and ask yourself:

- Where in your financial life do you feel stuck in either/or choices?
- What would it mean to know you could say yes to both sides of the decision?
- How would your peace of mind change if you knew your capital could keep growing even while you used it?

Write down one area where the AND Asset could free you from an either/or tradeoff. That simple exercise will shift how you see money.

The AND Asset is the defining feature of the Private Family Reserve. It transforms money from a scarce, single-use resource into a renewable, multi-use system, with one dollar doing two jobs and providing both growth and use, preservation and opportunity.

Chapter 11
Policy Loans: Borrowing Without Sacrificing Growth

The Power of Access

Two of the greatest financial frustrations in life are:

1. ***An emergency***, and no cash on hand to deal with it.
2. ***An opportunity***, and no cash available to seize it.

For most families and business owners, this is exactly the position they find themselves in. Even if they've built savings, those dollars are often locked away in registered accounts, tied up in investments, or exposed to tax consequences the moment they're accessed. The result? Stress, uncertainty, and missed opportunities.

Policy loans change this story. They allow you to access capital when you need it, quickly, privately, and on your terms, without interrupting the compounding growth of your Private Family Reserve. It's one of the most misunderstood but transformational features of Participating Whole Life Insurance policies.

How Policy Loans Work

When you need capital, you don't withdraw money from your policy. Instead, you borrow against it. Here's what that means:

- Your policy's cash value acts as collateral.
- The insurance company lends you its money, secured by your policy.
- Meanwhile, your cash value continues to grow uninterrupted inside the policy.

This simple design is the engine that powers the AND Asset. You can enjoy the fruit of your orchard today while the tree continues to grow for tomorrow. Unlike traditional accounts, where withdrawals permanently reduce growth potential, policy loans preserve uninterrupted compounding.

Key benefits include:

- **Liquidity:** Access funds within days, without penalty.
- **Privacy:** No credit checks, income verification, or invasive paperwork.
- **Control:** No fixed repayment schedule. You decide how and when to repay.
- **Flexibility:** Funds can be used for anything: business expansion, investment, education, emergencies, or opportunities.

In short, you've taken back the banking function. You no longer rely on external lending institutions that impose their rules and profit from your need for capital. You control the terms.

Why This Creates Unmatched Control

Policy loans solve a problem most families don't even realize they have: every time you spend a dollar, you give up all of the interest that dollar could have earned.

With policy loans, you're no longer forced into that tradeoff. You can borrow against your policy to make a purchase, and your capital continues compounding as if untouched. Yes, you'll pay interest on the loan, but unlike external lenders, you control the terms. And every repayment strengthens the overall pool, benefiting all policyholders, including you.

Compare the two experiences:

- **External Lending Institution Loan:** Paperwork, credit checks, fixed repayment schedules, late fees, and a system designed to benefit the lender's shareholders.

- **Policy Loan**: Simple request, no questions asked, proceeds in days, repayment entirely under your control, and growth uninterrupted.

This difference creates peace of mind. Emergencies no longer induce panic. Opportunities no longer slip away. The orchard keeps growing while you enjoy its fruit.

The Equipment Purchase

Consider a business owner, Rachel, who needs $150,000 for new equipment. In the past, she had two options: borrow from a lending institution at rigid terms, or pay cash and deplete her reserves. Either way, she gave up control.

But once Rachel established her Private Family Reserve, she had a third option. She borrowed against her policy. The process was simple, with no credit check, no questions, just a short request form. Within a week, she had the funds.

Her equipment was purchased, her business expanded, and, here's the key, her $150,000 of policy cash value continued to grow uninterrupted. She preserved her orchard and still enjoyed the harvest. Instead of an OR decision, she created an AND solution.

Real-World Applications

Policy loans are not limited to business use. They serve families in countless ways:

- **Education:** Parents borrow against policies to fund tuition while their cash value continues compounding for future needs.
- **Real Estate:** Investors use policy loans for down payments while their capital inside the policy keeps growing.
- **Emergencies:** Families cover medical costs or unexpected expenses without dipping into taxable accounts or triggering penalties.
- **Opportunities:** When the right investment arises, capital is available without waiting on approvals or liquidating assets.

Each use reinforces the same truth: policy loans transform money from a limited resource into a renewable system. The orchard keeps growing even as you enjoy the fruit.

Pause for a moment and consider:

- How many times have you wished you had quick access to capital?
- How many opportunities have you missed because your money was tied up, taxed, or unavailable?
- What would change if you could act instantly, knowing your orchard kept growing in the background?
- Write down one situation from your past, whether an emergency, an opportunity, or a major purchase, where a policy loan could have

given you peace of mind. This exercise will help you see just how valuable this feature can be.

Policy loans are the key that unlocks the full potential of the Private Family Reserve. They deliver liquidity without sacrifice, control without stress, and flexibility without compromise. They allow Wealth Creators to finance life on their own terms while preserving uninterrupted compounding.

And yet, the true magic of this system is not just what it does for you today; it's how it preserves and expands your orchard for generations to come. In the next chapter, we'll explore how this system ensures your family not only inherits wealth but also the method to keep the orchard flourishing long into the future.

Chapter 12

Cascading Life Insurance for Generational Wealth

Beyond Money – Passing Down a System

What if your children and grandchildren didn't just inherit money, but a system that ensured money would keep working for them long after you were gone?

Most families focus on leaving behind assets, such as an investment portfolio, a business, or real estate. Those can be valuable, but without a framework for stewardship, wealth often erodes within one or two generations. Taxes take a portion, poor decisions take another, and soon the orchard you spent your life cultivating is reduced to a few scattered trees.

Wealth Creators think differently. They don't just leave apples; they leave orchards. More importantly, they leave the orchard mindset: thriving systems designed to keep producing fruit for generations. Cascading life insurance is the tool that makes this possible.

Why Most Wealth Transfers Fail

History and research show a sobering truth: the majority of wealth doesn't survive beyond the second or third generation.

Why? *Three reasons:*

1. **Taxes:** The largest bill many families ever pay comes at death. Registered accounts are taxed in full on second death. Capital gains crystallize in taxable accounts. Taxes owed on the family business and on real estate can create serious liquidity issues. Without planning, orchards are cut down just to pay the tax man.

2. **Spending:** Without guidance, heirs often consume wealth rather than grow it. Apples are eaten, but no trees are planted.

3. **Knowledge Gap:** The most damaging loss isn't money, it's mindset. If heirs don't understand how wealth leaks away through taxes, negative returns, and capital transfers, they can't protect the orchard.

The result? Legacies evaporate quickly. Families who worked hard to build abundance leave behind only fleeting comfort, not enduring impact.

Planting Orchards for Generations

Cascading life insurance helps solve this by building a system that outlives you.

It works like this: instead of limiting the Private Family Reserve to your own lifetime, you establish policies on your children, and even your grandchildren. Each policy is a new tree planted in the family orchard.

- **While you're alive:** You control and benefit from the growth. Liquidity is available for opportunities or emergencies for you and your family.
- **Later in life, or at your passing:** ownership and control of the policies transfer tax-free to your children, along with the Wealth Creator mindset. They don't just inherit money; they inherit the knowledge and process to keep the orchard growing.

- **As your children mature:** they can continue contributing to the policies, especially by shifting funds from taxable accounts into a tax-exempt environment. They can also access policy loans for real needs like education, a first home, or launching a business, all while the policies keep compounding. And as they build families of their own, they can take out policies on their children too, expanding the orchard and ensuring the Wealth Creator mindset and system continues across generations.

- **When your children pass:** The death benefit flows tax-free to your grandchildren, who inherit not only capital but also the structure and mindset to keep the orchard growing.

Imagine that: with the stroke of a pen, you've created a system that impacts three generations, each one stronger than the last. This is the cascade, with capital flowing downwards, each layer feeding the next.

The Orchard in Action

Imagine you establish a Private Family Reserve and also start a policy on your child.

- Over the decades, both policies grow.

- You borrow against yours for business opportunities, while your child's policy quietly compounds in the background.

- When you graduate from this earth, your policy pays out a tax-free death benefit. That money can be directed into your child's policy, instantly boosting their reserve, or into a new policy for your grandchildren. In this way, the orchard doesn't just continue; it expands, ensuring the Wealth Creator system grows stronger with each generation.

- Your child inherits both liquidity and a working system, not just accounts or assets with no framework for how to use them.

The orchard has not only been preserved; it has been expanded.

Now, picture this cascading across multiple generations. Each layer plants new trees. Each harvest adds to the next. Instead of eroding, the family orchard compounds across time.

Pause here and consider:

- Do I want to leave behind only money, or also the framework for stewarding it?
- What would it mean if my grandchildren inherited not just assets, but a proven system that keeps compounding no matter what happens in the markets or tax code?
- Am I thinking in terms of one lifetime, or in terms of three generations and beyond?

These questions separate consumers from Wealth Creators. Consumers focus only on retirement. Wealth Creators focus on their family's future.

How Cascading Policies Plug the Leaks

Let's connect this strategy back to the three wealth leaks:

1. **Taxes:** Each policy grows in a tax-exempt environment. Death benefits pass down tax-free. The ticking tax time bomb is permanently defused.

2. **Negative Returns:** Policies do not go backward. Compounding is uninterrupted, generation after generation.

3. **Capital Transfers:** With policy loans, families borrow against policies instead of withdrawing, preserving growth while still accessing capital.

Cascading policies ensure that leaks aren't just plugged for one generation, but permanently sealed across many.

Everyday Applications

Cascading life insurance isn't abstract. It shows up in everyday family planning:

- **Education funding:** A policy on a child can grow into a reserve for education without interrupting compounding.

- **Family business continuity:** Liquidity from death benefits can provide capital to keep a business running, avoiding forced sales.

- **Multigenerational gifts:** Instead of leaving money that may be spent, policies provide a structured way to pass on resources that continue to grow.

- **Philanthropy:** Families who want impact beyond their own name can use cascading policies to fund charitable foundations for generations.

Every application comes back to one principle: keep the orchard alive, keep the trees growing, and let each generation add more.

The Golden Rule of Legacy

Those who control capital make the rules. By cascading policies, you ensure that your family, not outside institutions, holds the gold and therefore writes the rules.

Instead of heirs being dependent on lending institutions or markets, they inherit liquidity on their own terms. Instead of scrambling to pay taxes, they inherit tax-free capital. Instead of starting from scratch, they inherit a compounding orchard already in motion.

This is true legacy: not just wealth, but the wisdom and system to preserve it.

We've already talked about the two certainties in life: death and taxes. Our children and grandchildren will face both. They will earn incomes, start businesses, and wrestle with rising taxes in their lifetimes. And one day, just like us, they too will graduate from this earth.

That is why Wealth Creators act now. They equip their families with a tool to navigate taxes while living and to be prepared for the inevitable tax bill that arrives at life's end. With cascading life insurance, liquidity and cash are always available, tax-free, at the passing of anyone in the family.

Cascading life insurance addresses both certainties. It shields future generations from rising taxes during life, and it provides the liquidity needed when death brings the largest tax bill of all. It plants orchards for children and grandchildren. It passes down not just capital, but control. Not just money, but mindset.

This is how Wealth Creators think: they design systems that last, orchards that expand, and legacies that endure.

Your orchard doesn't have to end with you. It can cascade and flourish across generations. The choice is yours: will you leave behind apples… or orchards?

Chapter 13

Rethinking the Mortgage with The Smith Manoeuvre™

The Myth of the "Good Debt" Payoff

Most Canadians see their mortgage as an anchor to cut loose as quickly as possible. Extra payments. Lump sums. A race to zero.

But what if the very debt you're paying down could quietly fund your investments, create annual tax deductions, and help you grow wealth, all without putting in a single extra dollar beyond your monthly mortgage payment?

That's exactly what **The Smith Manoeuvre™** offers, a uniquely Canadian way to transform non-deductible mortgage debt into a wealth-building engine.

How It Works

Here's the simple rhythm:

- You make your regular mortgage payment.
- The principal you pay down becomes available to re-borrow through a re-advanceable mortgage.

- You re-invest that borrowed money into income-producing assets.
- The interest on that new investment loan is tax-deductible.

Over time, your mortgage balance converts from non-deductible debt into fully deductible debt, while your investment portfolio grows in the background.

In plain terms: you keep living in your home and making your mortgage payments as usual, but at the same time, you're creating a growing stream of tax deductions and building an investment portfolio, without putting in any new out-of-pocket cash.

Why Conventional Wisdom Fails

The standard playbook says:

1. **Debt is the enemy.** Eliminate it fast.
2. **Interest is wasted.** Every prepayment saves money.
3. **Peace of mind comes from being debt-free.**

If what you thought to be true about mortgages turned out not to be true, when would you want to know? Each of the above belief hides an opportunity cost:

- Prepaying locks capital into your walls, out of reach in emergencies.

- Paying down principal erases compounding your money could have earned elsewhere.
- Debt-free looks safe, until life happens and you realize security comes from liquidity, not just the absence of debt.

The end result? A house with no mortgage… but little else to show for it.

The Orchard Perspective

Think of your mortgage like a strong wind blowing through your orchard. You can resist it, straining to hold your ground until the storm finally passes; that's the "pay it off fast" approach.

Or you can harness the wind, letting it turn the wheel that waters your orchard. That's **The Smith Manoeuvre™**: turning what feels like a liability into an asset, a force that feeds your system instead of draining it.

Integrating the Private Family Reserve

The Smith Manoeuvre™ is powerful on its own. Combined with your **Private Family Reserve**, it becomes transformative.

- **The Smith Manoeuvre™** creates tax deductions while building investments.

- The **Private Family Reserve** gives you liquidity, use, and control of your capital.

Together, they help address the three financial leaks without sacrificing growth or access.

And later, you might choose to use policy loans from your Reserve to retire the mortgage entirely, on your terms, not the lending institution's. The point isn't debt versus no debt. The point is control.

Why Wealth Creators Choose This Path

Wealth Creators understand three truths about mortgages:

- **Debt isn't the enemy; lack of control is.** With liquidity and strategy, tax-deductible debt becomes a tool.

- **Peace of mind comes from access, not just ownership.** Liquidity matters more than bragging rights to being "debt-free."

- **The real goal is uninterrupted compounding.** Every dollar should keep working, no matter what your mortgage balance says.

The Smith Manoeuvre™, paired with the **Private Family Reserve**, delivers on all three.

For decades, families were told the fastest path to security was paying off the mortgage. But racing to zero isn't wealth creation, it's just relief.

Wealth Creators see mortgages differently. They integrate them into a system, turning liabilities into assets, OR decisions into AND opportunities, and dead weight into living orchards that keep producing.

The Smith Manoeuvre™ is more than a clever tax play. It's proof that even your largest liability can become a tool for compounding, control, and peace of mind.

Your orchard doesn't have to shrink to pay off the mortgage. It can keep growing if you let every dollar do more than one job.

Chapter 14
Common Objections, Reframes, and Mental Breakthroughs

The Voice in Your Head

By now, you may be nodding along with much of what you've read. The orchard metaphor makes sense, the leaks are real, and the Private Family Reserve feels compelling.

And yet, there's a voice in your head.

It says things like: "What's the rate of return?" or "This sounds too good to be true. If it works, why isn't everyone doing it?"

That voice is normal. It's the sound of decades of conventional wisdom bumping against a new framework. The goal of this chapter isn't to silence that voice, but to engage it, to take each objection seriously and reframe it through the Wealth Creator lens.

Objections Are Invitations

Skepticism isn't a problem. In fact, it's healthy. When handled with respect, objections become invitations for deeper clarity.

Every family and business owner reaches this point. They've been taught to measure success by rates of return, to fear premiums, to pay down debt aggressively, to trust in registered accounts, or to believe that if something isn't mainstream, it must be flawed.

This chapter takes those mental roadblocks one by one. You'll see that the very concerns holding you back are often proof you're asking the right questions.

Objection 1: "What's the Rate of Return?"

It's the most common question, but it's the wrong place to start.

Reframe: The question isn't how much your money earns, but how much you control.

Think about it. What asset do you believe delivers the best return? Equities? Crypto? Alternatives? How confident are you that asset will be performing well ten years from now, or even in the very year you need the money? The truth is, no one knows.

Now imagine that in that exact year, an emergency strikes or a once-in-a-lifetime opportunity appears... and your chosen asset is down 30%. What good is a "high return" if the account you need most is underwater?

Take it further. Imagine markets across the board are down: stocks, bonds, even real estate. Lending institutions are pulling back, credit is tight, and liquidity is scarce. Where do you turn then?

That's why control matters more than return. The critical question isn't, "What's my rate of return?" It's, "What's the rate of return on cash I can access, tax-free, on demand, in the very year when everything else is down and I need it most?"

That return isn't measured in percentages. It's measured in peace of mind, opportunities seized, and disasters avoided. In those moments, the return is immeasurable. The best investment is the one that pays the most, when you need it the most!

Still, you may want to own a particular asset, such as real estate, a business expansion, or a market opportunity. That's fine. With the Private Family Reserve, you don't have to choose between safety and opportunity. This is the AND Asset: you can do both.

Scenario 1: Investing without the Private Family Reserve

You put your dollars directly into the investment. On paper, it looks simple:

- Gross yield
- Less taxes = **Net yield**

Scenario 2: Investing with the Private Family Reserve

Now compare that to running the same dollars through your Participating Whole Life Insurance policy first, then borrowing against the policy to buy the investment:

- Gross yield
- Less policy loan interest = Taxable gain
- Less taxes = Net yield from the investment

But here's the key: *you also own the policy itself which earns income on a tax-advantaged basis.* The total outcome looks like this:

- Net yield from the investment (above) + Net yield from the Private Family Reserve = Total yield

This principle applies to any investment you might make. Which is why no one can ever achieve a "higher rate of return" by ignoring the banking process.

Objection 2: "The Premiums Are Expensive."

Have you ever heard someone say, "I just added $7,000 to my TFSA; that was expensive!" Or, "I just invested $50,000 into a stock; wow, what an expense!" Of course not. Why? Because they view those contributions as investments, not costs. They know the money is still theirs and can be accessed if needed.

Policyholders see premiums the same way. They're eager to add money each year because they know it will grow, compound, and earn interest daily for the rest of their lives, while still remaining accessible for opportunities or emergencies.

More importantly, policyholders understand the real issues: the three leaks we've already uncovered. And here's the key, if you don't understand the problem, the solution won't do you any good.

That's why Wealth Creators never view premiums as the problem. **The premium is the solution to the problem.**

Objection 3: "Why Borrow Against My Policy When Bank Loans Are Cheaper?"

A lending institution might advertise a lower interest rate, so why not just go there?

Reframe: The question isn't about cost; it's about control.

External loans come with applications, credit checks, and rigid repayment schedules. A policy loan requires none of those. You choose how and when to repay. And while you borrow, your entire cash value keeps compounding uninterrupted.

That benefit far outweighs the interest rate comparison. It's not about finding the cheapest loan; it's about having the most flexible and reliable source of capital, one that works for you no matter what.

Objection 4: "What If I Can't Keep Contributing?"

Life changes. Incomes fluctuate. Families wonder if they'll be locked into a rigid obligation.

Reframe: Properly designed policies are built for flexibility.

You're not trapped. There are options to reduce, pause, or restructure contributions. Unlike mortgages or loans, policy funding isn't a hard-edged contract that punishes you. It's a design you control, scaled to your needs.

And consider the opposite. What if you experience a windfall, higher income, or new wealth and want to add more money to your system? Your orchard can grow. As your capacity increases, you can add more policies, each one sheltering and compounding additional capital inside your Private Family Reserve.

Here's the key: every day, we move closer to the point where we may no longer be insurable. But once your policies are in place, they can never be taken away. Even if your health changes, you can keep contributing to your existing policies and expanding your orchard.

Objection 5: "Isn't This Too Good to Be True? Why Isn't Everyone Doing It?"

This is one of the most common questions, and it makes sense.

Reframe: The reason many people don't do this is simple: they've never been shown how.

In reality, countless prominent business owners and families are already using this exact strategy. The Private Family Reserve isn't some new invention; it's a fresh perspective on a century-old tool that has quietly created stability and wealth for those who've discovered it.

The fact that it isn't mainstream doesn't make it flawed; it simply means the mainstream hasn't caught up yet.

Objection 6: "What If the Insurance Company Goes Bankrupt?"

Trusting a policy requires trusting the company.

Reframe: Participating whole life is built on some of the most stable institutions in history.

Life insurance companies are regulated conservatively, with reserves and safeguards far beyond most financial institutions. For over 150 years, through depressions, wars, and recessions, these companies have delivered uninterrupted growth. This track record provides lasting reassurance for policyholders.

Objection 7: "Buy Term and Invest the Difference."

This advice is repeated often by financial entertainers. The logic sounds simple: buy cheap term insurance, invest the savings elsewhere, and you'll come out ahead.

Reframe: Term insurance expires. Wealth Creator strategies are permanent.

Yes, term may look cheaper in the early years, but costs climb dramatically later, and at some point, the coverage disappears, often when you need it most. Meanwhile, "investing the difference" usually means exposing capital to taxes and volatility, the very leaks that quietly erode wealth.

Buying term and investing the difference doesn't solve the three leaks. In many cases, it makes them worse.

Objection 8: "The Advisor Gets Paid Too Much."

Some people worry this system benefits the advisor more than the family.

Reframe: Now that you understand the three most vexing wealth-building problems, taxes, negative returns, and capital transfers, ask yourself: *what is the solution worth to you?* The answer is simple: it's invaluable.

Yes, the advisor gets paid. But your family reaps the benefits: uninterrupted growth, liquidity, tax efficiency, and a legacy that can impact several generations. That's why it's essential to be coached by an Authorized IBC Practitioner from the Nelson Nash Institute who not only teaches this process but also **lives it themselves** and has years of experience guiding families to become their own banker.

Experience and excellence aren't expensive; they're priceless.

Objection 9: "What If the Tax Rules Change?"

Canada's tax laws can and do shift. Families worry about planning around rules that may not last.

Reframe: Rules can change, but Wealth Creators design systems that are resilient to change.

The Private Family Reserve is not built on fragile loopholes. It rests on longstanding tax treatment for insurance that has survived political shifts for over a century. Even if rules change, the fundamental advantage, tax-exempt growth inside the policy, has proven durable. And unlike registered accounts, where deferred taxes can explode at death, the policy pays tax-free benefits precisely when families need them most.

Objection 10: "I don't have any children, I don't need insurance."

Whether you have children or not, the same truth applies. You still have to solve for the three financial leaks, taxes, negative returns, and capital transfers. Your money still has to reside somewhere. The question is: what's the best home for it?

Becoming a Wealth Creator is not just about leaving an inheritance. It is about controlling the banking function in your life and solving the three problems that quietly erode wealth. The death benefit is the cherry on top, but the real value is in the cake: uninterrupted compounding, liquidity, and control during your lifetime.

You can leave the death benefit to any cause or person you choose, whether family, charity, or community. Either way, the strategy serves you first, and those you care about second.

Objection 11: "I am too old. I'm not insurable"

Even if you're not personally insurable, you can still build your Private Family Reserve. You can be the owner of the policy while the life insured is someone else: a spouse, a business partner, a child, or even a grandchild.

In other words, there are many ways to get your orchard off the ground. Ownership gives you control of the policy and access to the capital, regardless of whose life is insured. The orchard can still grow, and you can still enjoy its fruit.

Skepticism is natural. It means you're paying attention. But when you look deeper, each objection collapses under the weight of truth:

- It's not about return; it's about control.
- Premiums aren't the problem; they are the solution.
- Interest isn't the enemy; loss of compounding is.
- Flexibility is built in.
- Mainstream doesn't equal correct.
- Stability is proven.
- Term is temporary.
- Advisor alignment matters.
- Tax rules change, but systems endure.

The shift is simple but profound: from fear to clarity, doubt to confidence, and consumer thinking to Wealth Creator thinking.

Your orchard is waiting. The leaks are plugged. The questions have answers. The objections have become breakthroughs.

Now it's time to see the full orchard vision in action.

Chapter 15
From Seed to Orchard: The Wealth Creator's Conclusion

It All Begins with a Seed

Every orchard begins the same way, with a single seed placed in the ground.

That seed doesn't look like much at first. It's small, fragile, and easy to overlook. Yet inside it lives the blueprint for something vast: roots that stretch deep, branches that climb high, and fruit that feeds families for generations.

Your financial life is no different. For years, you've been told to chase returns, pay cash, defer taxes, or "ride out" the markets. Those ideas may have felt safe, but they left your bucket leaking and your orchard exposed.

Now, you've seen another way. You've discovered that the real power lies not in chasing balloons or chopping down trees, but in planting, protecting, and growing an orchard that lasts.

The Journey So Far

Let's take a breath and trace the path you've walked in these pages.

- You saw the **three leaks** that erode wealth: taxes draining fruit year after year, negative returns breaking the compounding chain, and capital transfers chopping down trees for one-time gains.

- You imagined the **ideal account**: tax-exempt, liquid, compounding without interruption, and proven through history.

- You learned that such an account already exists, a carefully designed Participating Whole Life Insurance policy, your **Private Family Reserve.**

- You walked through the **7-Step Transformation,** moving from awareness to action.

- You discovered advanced applications: how dollars can do two jobs at once with the **AND Asset,** how **policy loans** give you control and liquidity, how **cascading policies** plant orchards for your children, and even how to rethink the **mortgage trap** with **The Smith Manoeuvre™.**

- Finally, you faced the **common objections** that naturally arise and reframed them into breakthroughs that built confidence instead of doubt.

Each chapter was a step. Each step created a shift. And together, they've led you here, to the orchard vision.

From Consumer to Wealth Creator

The biggest change isn't the tool. It's you.

At the start, you may have seen yourself as a consumer of financial products, waiting for the newest golf club and hoping it would improve your game. Now you know the truth: it's not about the club. It's about the swing. It's about mindset.

Wealth Creators think differently. They don't chase after higher returns. They don't hand control to outside institutions. They don't accept leaks as inevitable.

They focus on **control, clarity, and compounding.** They protect their trees, plug their leaks, and plant orchards for generations. They step into the role of banker in their own lives, and they find peace, not stress, when it comes to money.

That's who you're becoming.

The Peace of the Orchard

Think for a moment about what this shift delivers:

- **Peace of mind today.** Emergencies no longer mean panic. Opportunities no longer slip by. You have liquidity on your terms.
- **Compounding without interruption.** Your money grows steadily, safely, every single day.
- **Freedom from the retirement gamble.** Market drops and tax hikes no longer hold power over you.
- **A true legacy.** Not just money, but a mindset. Not just apples, but an orchard that endures.

This is what it feels like to move from chasing to cultivating, from consuming to creating, from worrying to resting.

Pause and ask yourself:

- Which leaks have I been ignoring, and how much could I save by plugging them now?
- What would it feel like to never interrupt compounding again?
- How would my family's future change if I stopped chopping down trees and instead expanded the orchard for the next generation?
- If not now, when?

These questions are the bridge between learning and acting. Transformation isn't about waiting for perfect conditions; it's about planting seeds today.

Planting Today for Tomorrow's Harvest

The best time to plant a tree was 20 years ago. The second-best time is today.

The same is true for your Private Family Reserve. Every day you delay is a day of compounding lost, a season when the orchard could have grown larger. Every day you wait is another apple handed to the tax man, another storm left to break your compounding chain, another tree cut down for one-time cash.

But the moment you begin, the moment you plant, the cycle shifts. Growth begins. Peace arrives. Legacy takes root.

It all began with a seed. That seed was an idea: that you don't have to chase, guess, or gamble with money. That you can control it, grow it, and protect it. That you can stop leaks, preserve trees, and plant orchards that feed your family for generations.

Now the seed has been planted in you. The question is whether you will let it grow.

This isn't about someday; it's about today. Right now, you have the chance to move from consumer to Wealth Creator. To build a **Private Family Reserve**. To create peace of mind for yourself and legacy for your family.

Your orchard is waiting. The leaks can be plugged. The fruit can stay in your family. The harvest can feed generations.

All it takes is the decision to plant, and to keep planting, until the orchard is full.

Because when you plant with vision, you don't just change your financial future. You change your family's story.

www.ingramcontent.com/pod-product-compliance
Lightning Source LLC
LaVergne TN
LVHW022105200926
848481LV00003B/1064